SHADOWS OF THE MIND: UNDERSTANDING DARK PSYCHOLOGY AND MANIPULATION

Unraveling the Techniques, Intentions and Defenses in the Hidden World of Persuasion

By

Nathan Miller

Table of Contents

INTRODUCTION

In the intricate tapestry of human behavior, there exists a shadowy realm, a subset of psychological tactics and strategies often used to control, influence, and manipulate. This hidden dimension, known as dark psychology, has existed for millennia but remains largely unexplored in popular literature. It's a place where power plays aren't merely games but art forms, where influence transcends simple persuasion, morphing into covert manipulation. "Shadows of the Mind: Understanding Dark Psychology and Manipulation" seeks to illuminate this enigmatic world, offering readers a comprehensive guide to its depths and nuances.

Dark psychology isn't inherently evil; it's a tool, much like a knife, which can be used for harm or for culinary artistry. The intent behind its application determines its impact. Some use it to control and exploit, while others may inadvertently use aspects of it, unaware of the repercussions. This book does not aim to vilify, but to educate, to bring awareness, and to empower.

Over the centuries, philosophers, psychologists, and scholars have tried to dissect and understand the motives behind manipulation. Why do some individuals seek to control others? What pleasures or rewards do they derive from it? These questions are not easily answered, but our journey begins by attempting to discern the mindset of the manipulator.

As the digital era ushers in unprecedented levels of connectivity, new avenues for manipulation emerge. Traditional face-to-face manipulative tactics have evolved, adapting to the realm of screens and online personas. This book ventures into such adaptations, drawing connections between age-old tactics and their modern counterparts.

By embarking on this journey, you're not just equipping yourself with the knowledge to understand dark psychology; you're taking steps to safeguard your mental and emotional well-being. Knowledge, as they say, is power. By understanding the mechanisms of manipulation, one can recognize its onset, resist its effects, and reclaim one's autonomy.

It's essential to remember that dark psychology is but one facet of the vast spectrum of human behavior. Just as there are those who might wield its tactics with ill intent, countless others believe in building connections based on trust, understanding, and genuine affection. By confronting and understanding the shadows, we can better appreciate the light.

Welcome to "Shadows of the Mind." Prepare to delve deep, to challenge your perceptions, and to emerge with newfound knowledge and clarity. Let's embark on this enlightening journey together.

CHAPTER ONE

The Hidden Face of Influence

The Intricate Web of Dark Psychology

At the very heart of human interaction lies the potential for influence. Influence, in its simplest form, is the ability to affect the thoughts, behaviors, or feelings of others. But when this influence crosses into the realm of dark psychology, it becomes a subtle and often undetected form of manipulation. This chapter delves into the foundations of dark psychology, revealing its hidden face in everyday life and setting the stage for a deeper understanding of manipulation in its various forms.

Understanding Dark Psychology

Dark psychology is the study of the human condition as it relates to the psychological nature of people to prey upon others. It encompasses the part of human behavior that involves the use and abuse of power over others. This is not a topic that exists only in the realms of crime or within the halls of psychiatric institutions. Rather, it is a day-to-day occurrence, often so subtle and deeply woven into our interactions that it goes unnoticed.

Manipulation, a core component of dark psychology, can be seen in numerous settings: from a salesperson employing high-pressure tactics to a partner using emotional blackmail in a relationship. It's a multifaceted tool, applied in ways that can be straightforward or intricately complex.

The Evolution of Manipulation

Manipulation is as old as human interactions themselves. From ancient rhetoricians who mastered the art of persuasion to today's sophisticated digital influencers, the evolution of manipulation mirrors the evolution of society and communication. In ancient times, understanding and influencing public opinion were skills as critical as they are today.

In modern times, with the advent of psychology as a science, we began to understand these tactics not just as art or instinct but as processes that have a basis in human psychology. The 20th century, particularly with the rise of mass media, saw manipulation tactics used en masse, from advertising to political propaganda.

Everyday Manipulation: Hidden in Plain Sight

Manipulation in everyday life often goes unnoticed because it is so ingrained in our daily interactions. Whether it's the subtle influence of advertising, the persuasive pitch of a salesperson, or even the way family members interact, manipulation can take many forms. Recognizing these forms is the first step in understanding dark psychology.

1. **Advertising and Consumer Behavior:** Advertisements often use psychological tactics such as appealing to emotions, creating a sense of urgency, or using authority figures to influence consumer behavior.

2. **Workplace Dynamics:** From office politics to authoritative leadership styles, manipulation can manifest in various forms in the workplace, often influencing decision-making processes and team dynamics.

3. **Interpersonal Relationships:** This includes the use of guilt, obligation, gaslighting, or charm to control or influence partners, friends, or family members.

The Psychology Behind Manipulation

Understanding the psychological mechanisms that make manipulation possible is crucial. Human beings are susceptible to a range of cognitive biases and emotional triggers. Manipulators often exploit these biases and triggers. Some of these include:

- **Reciprocity:** The desire to return favors or maintain a balance in social exchanges.
- **Commitment and Consistency:** Once people commit to something, they are more likely to go through with it.
- **Social Proof:** People tend to do things they see others doing.
- **Authority:** People tend to obey authority figures.
- **Liking:** People are easily influenced by someone they like.
- **Scarcity:** Perceived scarcity will generate demand.

Recognizing the Signs

Recognizing manipulation involves understanding these psychological triggers and being mindful of when they are being exploited. It's not always easy, as manipulation can be very subtle. Here are some signs:

- **Emotional Pressure:** Feeling guilt-tripped, scared, or unduly obligated.
- **Inconsistencies:** Noticing discrepancies in what the manipulator says and does.
- **Isolation:** Being cut off from other perspectives or support networks.
- **Gaslighting:** Feeling like your reality or memories are being questioned or altered.

Conclusion of Chapter 1

As we close this chapter, it's vital to acknowledge that understanding and identifying manipulation in its many forms is the first step in demystifying dark psychology. Recognizing these tactics in our daily lives empowers us to make more informed decisions and protect our mental and emotional well-being. In the upcoming chapters, we will delve deeper into the minds of manipulators, explore various manipulation tactics in different areas of life, and learn how to effectively counter these strategies. This journey is not just about uncovering the hidden faces of influence but also about reclaiming our own power in the dynamic landscape of human interaction.

CHAPTER TWO

Psychology of the Manipulator

Prologue: The Enigmatic Architect of Influence

At the heart of every act of manipulation is an individual: the manipulator. Understanding this central figure is akin to deciphering the blueprint of a maze. Their motives, desires, and techniques form the walls and pathways that often trap the unsuspecting. This chapter aims to dissect the mindset, traits, and motivations behind those who engage in manipulative behaviors, offering a comprehensive portrait of the manipulator.

The Mind of a Manipulator: An Overview

Manipulators are not always overtly malicious or even aware of their manipulative tendencies. They can range from the intentionally deceptive to those who have unconsciously developed manipulative habits as a means of survival or communication. Their motivations can be as diverse as seeking power, wanting attention, or merely desiring control over their environment.

Fundamental Traits of Manipulators

While manipulators can vary widely in their methods and motives, some fundamental traits are commonly exhibited among them:

1. **Lack of Responsibility:** They rarely admit their faults and are quick to blame others.
2. **Skilled Liar:** Whether it's a white lie or a web of deceit, manipulators are adept at bending the truth.
3. **Charm and Charisma:** Their likable persona can draw people in, making their influence more potent.
4. **Intense Need for Control:** They often need to feel in control of their surroundings, events, and especially people.
5. **Lack of Empathy:** While they may understand emotions (to exploit them), they often lack genuine empathy for others.

Deep-Seated Motivations

Several underlying motivations drive manipulators:

1. **Power and Dominance:** For some, the thrill is in having power over others, dictating their thoughts, emotions, and actions.
2. **Emotional Void:** Some manipulators seek to fill an emotional void by drawing attention or emotions (like sympathy) from others.
3. **Personal Gain:** Whether it's money, status, or material items, some manipulate purely for tangible benefits.
4. **Insecurity and Fear:** Surprisingly, many manipulators are driven by their insecurities, using manipulation as a defense mechanism.

The Spectrum of Manipulation: From Subtle to Sinister

Manipulators exist on a spectrum, with some being relatively benign and others possessing a sinister intent. On one end are individuals who might use manipulation unconsciously, born out of habit or coping mechanisms. On the other end are those who employ manipulation with full awareness and intent, often for personal gain at the expense of others.

The Interplay of Nature and Nurture

The age-old debate of nature versus nurture also finds relevance in the world of manipulation. Some manipulators may have genetic predispositions, like traits associated with narcissism or sociopathy. However, upbringing, childhood experiences, and environmental factors play an equally crucial role in molding a manipulator.

Manipulators and Relationships

Manipulators often reveal their true nature in the context of relationships:

1. **Romantic Relationships:** They might use tactics like love-bombing (overwhelming affection followed by cold withdrawal) or gaslighting.
2. **Family Dynamics:** Parent-child or sibling relationships can be rife with manipulation, often rooted in established patterns from childhood.
3. **Friendships:** Manipulators often position themselves as indispensable friends, only to leverage this perceived closeness later.

Tactics of the Trade

Understanding a manipulator requires an exploration of their techniques:

- **Emotional Manipulation:** Using emotions as levers, from guilt-tripping to invoking jealousy.
- **Verbal Influence:** Employing persuasive language or double speak to confuse or control.
- **Withholding:** This can be in the form of affection, approval, or information to create a power imbalance.
- **Playing the Victim:** Positioning themselves as the aggrieved party to elicit sympathy or concessions.

Countering the Manipulative Mindset

While this chapter delves deep into the psyche of manipulators, it's essential not to feel powerless or overly cynical about human interactions. Recognizing the signs and understanding the mindset are the first steps in countering manipulative behavior. Armed with this knowledge, one can establish boundaries, seek supportive environments, and engage in open communication to reduce the manipulator's influence.

Chapter's Epilogue: A Mosaic of Human Complexity

Manipulators, with all their intricacies, are a part of the vast mosaic of human behavior and psychology. By understanding them, we not only protect ourselves but also perhaps offer avenues for genuine understanding and change. As we proceed, remember that every manipulator is also a human, shaped by a myriad of experiences and factors. The aim is not to demonize but to understand, adapt, and grow.

In subsequent chapters, we will further explore the tools in the manipulator's arsenal and provide strategies to recognize, resist, and counteract their influence. The journey into the shadows continues, but with each step, we inch closer to enlightenment and empowerment.

CHAPTER THREE

Tools of Deception: A Deep Dive into Manipulative Tactics

Introduction: The Many Masks of Manipulation

If understanding the mind of the manipulator was akin to unveiling the architect, this chapter seeks to understand the tools they employ to build their world of deception. Every manipulator, while distinct in motive and method, draws from a shared arsenal of tactics. By understanding these tools, we are better equipped to identify and protect against them.

The Landscape of Manipulative Tactics

Manipulation is often more art than science, with tactics tailored to individual situations and targets. However, at their core, these tactics exploit universal human vulnerabilities, whether emotional, cognitive, or social.

1. Emotional Leverage

Guilt Tripping: By making someone feel guilty, a manipulator can get them to act against their best interests. For instance, statements like "After all I've done for you, you owe me this" is a classic example.

Fear and Intimidation: Employing threats, whether overt or covert, to make someone comply. This could range from physical threats to subtler ones like threatening to reveal embarrassing information.

Love Bombing: Overwhelming someone with affection and praise to make them dependent and then suddenly withdrawing, creating a cycle of dependency.

2. Cognitive Exploits

Gaslighting: Making someone doubt their own reality, memories, or perceptions. A manipulator might deny previous statements or actions, making the other person question their sanity.

Overloading with Information: Bombarding someone with arguments, facts, or data, often irrelevant, to overwhelm and confuse them.

Deflection: Avoiding accountability by redirecting conversations or blaming others.

3. Social Dynamics

Bandwagon Effect: Convincing someone to do something because "everyone else is doing it."

Social Proof: Using the actions or opinions of others to validate a particular choice or behavior.

Divide and Rule: Creating rifts between individuals to ensure they don't unite against the manipulator.

The Subtleties of Verbal Manipulation

Language is one of the manipulator's most potent tools. How they phrase statements, the words they choose, and the tone they employ can all be tailored to influence and control.

Leading Questions: Questions framed to lead someone to a particular conclusion, e.g., "Don't you think it's time you moved on?"

Double Bind: Offering choices that all lead to the same outcome. It gives the illusion of choice when there's none.

Ambiguity: Using vague language to avoid commitment or to be able to change stance later.

The Role of Non-Verbal Cues

Manipulation isn't solely verbal. Non-verbal cues play a vital role:

Mirroring: Adopting someone's body language, gestures, or tone to create a sense of similarity and trust.

Intimidating Presence: Using physical posture or proximity to assert dominance or create discomfort.

Selective Attention: Giving or withholding attention to reward or punish behavior.

Digital Age Deception

The digital era has given birth to new avenues of manipulation:

Online Echo Chambers: Encouraging individuals to stay in environments where only their viewpoints are echoed back, fostering a skewed sense of reality.

Misinformation and Fake News: Spreading false information to shape opinions.

Cyberbullying and Online Intimidation: Using the cloak of anonymity to harass or intimidate.

Protecting Against Manipulative Tactics

Awareness is the primary defense against manipulation. By recognizing these tactics:

1. **Establish Boundaries:** Know your limits and communicate them clearly.
2. **Seek External Perspectives:** Outside perspectives can offer clarity.
3. **Practice Assertiveness:** Being able to express your feelings and rights respectfully and firmly can counter manipulation.
4. **Educate Yourself:** Knowledge about these tactics is empowering.

Chapter's Conclusion: Mastery over Manipulation

By understanding the tools in the manipulator's toolkit, we can navigate interactions with clarity and confidence. While the world of manipulation may seem daunting, equipped with awareness and understanding, one can not only guard against these tactics but also foster genuine, open, and healthy interactions.

In the upcoming chapters, we'll delve into real-life scenarios, case studies, and practical strategies to handle manipulators across different contexts. From personal relationships to the workplace, the journey towards understanding and empowerment continues.

CHAPTER FOUR

Shadows in the Mind: Recognizing and Understanding Dark Triad Traits

Introduction: The Ominous Trinity of Personality

When delving into the realm of manipulation and dark psychology, one cannot overlook the infamous 'Dark Triad' – a triad that comprises narcissism, Machiavellianism, and psychopathy. These traits, while different in their nuances, often overlap and converge in ways that foster manipulative behaviors. In this extensive exploration, we aim to offer a comprehensive understanding of these traits, their intersections, and their manifestations in daily life.

The Framework of the Dark Triad

Before delving deep, it's essential to clarify the framework:

1. **Narcissism:** Characterized by grandiosity, entitlement, dominance, and superiority.
2. **Machiavellianism:** Marked by manipulation, cynicism, and a focus on self-interest and deception.
3. **Psychopathy:** Identified by impulsiveness, thrill-seeking, and a lack of empathy and remorse.

1. Narcissism: The Ego's Echo

Origins and Manifestations: Rooted in Greek mythology where Narcissus fell in love with his reflection, modern narcissism isn't merely about vanity. It's a complex trait involving a fragile self-esteem, a need for admiration, and often, a lack of empathy.

Subtypes of Narcissism:

- **Grandiose Narcissism:** Outgoing, attention-seeking, and extremely confident. They desire admiration and often view themselves as superior.
- **Vulnerable Narcissism:** More sensitive and often harbor inner feelings of inadequacy. They may react strongly to criticism and feel envious.

Narcissism in Daily Interactions: From monopolizing conversations to seeking constant validation on social media, narcissistic tendencies can manifest subtly.

2. Machiavellianism: The Puppeteer's Strings

Origins and Manifestations: Named after Niccolò Machiavelli, who wrote "The Prince", a guide on political manipulation. Individuals with high Machiavellian traits view manipulation as a game and are often detached from traditional morality.

Machiavellian Tactics:

- **Strategic Planning:** They always think several steps ahead.
- **Exploitation:** Willingness to exploit others for personal gain.
- **Emotional Detachment:** Emotions rarely cloud their judgment; they operate on logic and strategy.

Machiavellianism in Social Contexts: From strategic networking to feigning friendships for personal advantages, Machiavellian traits can reshape social dynamics.

3. Psychopathy: The Abyss of Empathy

Origins and Understanding: Unlike the portrayal in popular culture, not all psychopaths are violent criminals. Psychopathy is a spectrum, and many high-functioning psychopaths navigate society seamlessly.

Characteristics of Psychopathy:

- **Shallow Emotions:** Limited emotional range, especially when it comes to understanding others' feelings.
- **Impulsivity:** Tendency to act without forethought.
- **Charming but Deceptive:** Often charismatic but use it for deceit.

Everyday Psychopathy: The smooth-talking con artist, the seemingly sincere lover with multiple affairs, or even the corporate leader with ruthless ambition, the manifestations are diverse.

Intersections of the Dark Triad

While these traits are distinct, they often overlap:

- A narcissistic individual might employ Machiavellian tactics to maintain their self-image.
- A psychopath, devoid of deep emotional connections, might manipulate others (Machiavellianism) to achieve their goals without any guilt.

The Dark Triad and Manipulation

The triad forms a potent recipe for manipulation. The narcissist's need for validation, the Machiavellian's strategic maneuvers, and the psychopath's lack of remorse can combine in various ways to influence and control others.

Spotting the Dark Triad in the Wild

Key signs include:

1. **Consistent Patterns of Manipulative Behavior:** Manipulation isn't an occasional tactic; it's a way of life.
2. **Lack of Genuine Emotional Depth:** Emotions are often surface-level or feigned for manipulation.
3. **Strategic Relationships:** Relationships are rarely genuine but often have a purpose or end goal.

Coping and Protecting Against the Dark Triad

1. **Awareness:** Recognizing these traits is the first step.
2. **Setting Boundaries:** Essential to protect oneself from undue influence.
3. **Seeking Support:** Discussing concerns with trusted individuals or professionals can offer perspective.

Conclusion: Navigating the Shadows

Understanding the Dark Triad offers insights into some of the most intricate and challenging aspects of human psychology. These traits, while ominous in their nature, are crucial to recognize, understand, and navigate. As we journey deeper into the realms of dark psychology in subsequent chapters, remember that knowledge is power, and understanding is the first step toward empowerment.

The subsequent chapters will delve deeper into the practical aspects, offering real-life examples, strategies, and coping mechanisms to handle individuals with high Dark Triad traits in various contexts, from personal relationships to professional environments. The voyage into the enigmatic continues, but with each page, we stride closer to clarity and mastery.

CHAPTER FIVE

Unraveling Influence: The Psychology of Persuasion and Control

Introduction: The Power of Persuasion

Persuasion is a tool older than civilization itself. From the first trades to modern marketing campaigns, the ability to influence others is a valuable skill. Yet, when infused with dark psychological underpinnings, it becomes a formidable weapon. This extensive chapter not only examines the mechanisms of persuasion but also dives deep into its darker manifestations.

The Art and Science of Persuasion

Persuasion can be both an art and a science:

- **Art:** The finesse, the timing, the ability to weave a narrative.
- **Science:** The psychological principles, the tested methods, the repeated patterns.

The Six Pillars of Persuasion by Dr. Robert Cialdini

Dr. Robert Cialdini, in his pioneering work, identified six fundamental principles of persuasion:

1. **Reciprocity:** People feel obligated to return a favor.
2. **Commitment and Consistency:** Once we commit to something, we're more likely to follow through.
3. **Social Proof:** We look to others to determine our behavior.
4. **Authority:** We tend to obey figures of authority.
5. **Liking:** We're more easily persuaded by people we like.
6. **Scarcity:** We value things that are scarce more than those in abundance.

Each principle, while innocuous on its own, can be weaponized for manipulative purposes.

Weaponizing Persuasion: Dark Tactics

1. Exploiting Reciprocity: Manipulators might offer unsolicited help, only to later guilt-trip you into doing something for them.

2. Abusing Commitment: By making someone commit verbally or in writing, a manipulator can later pressure them to follow through, even if circumstances change.

3. Manufacturing Social Proof: From fake online reviews to orchestrated peer pressure, manipulators can create a facade of social validation.

4. Feigned Authority: By projecting themselves as experts or using false credentials, manipulators gain undeserved trust.

5. Artificial Likability: Manipulators can feign interests, mirror behaviors, or use flattery to create a facade of likability.

6. Manufactured Scarcity: From "limited-time offers" to feigning high demand, creating an artificial sense of scarcity can rush decisions.

Subliminal Persuasion: The Silent Whisperer

Beyond overt tactics, persuasion can operate beneath conscious awareness:

- **Priming:** Introducing an idea or theme in subtle ways, making someone more receptive to related ideas later.

- **Anchoring:** The first piece of information encountered (an "anchor") influences subsequent judgments.

Digital Domains: The New Age Arenas of Persuasion

In an interconnected world, digital platforms offer new avenues for persuasion:

1. **Retargeted Ads:** Tracking online behavior to tailor persuasive messages.
2. **Social Media Echo Chambers:** Feeding individuals information that aligns with their beliefs, reinforcing those beliefs.
3. **Influencer Endorsements:** Leveraging the trust and admiration influencers command over their followers.

The Interplay of Persuasion and Dark Triad Traits

Manipulative individuals, particularly those with high Machiavellianism, often employ persuasion as a primary tool:

- A narcissist might use likability, showcasing their best traits to win people over.
- Machiavellians might create scenarios of artificial scarcity to make others act against their best interests.
- Psychopaths, with their charm, can employ authority and likability simultaneously, making their persuasion potent.

Guarding Against Dark Persuasion

Awareness is the first line of defense. Additional strategies include:

1. **Critical Thinking:** Always question the motives and the context.
2. **Seek Multiple Sources:** Especially true for information or decisions based on authority or social proof.
3. **Trust Your Instincts:** If something feels off, pause and reassess.

Conclusion: Navigating the Nuances

Persuasion, in essence, is not malevolent. It becomes a matter of concern when intertwined with manipulation and dark intent. Understanding its mechanisms, recognizing its manifestations, and developing defenses against its darker uses is imperative.

As we proceed in this exploration, the focus will shift from the abstract to the concrete, from understanding to action. The subsequent chapters will provide hands-on strategies, real-life scenarios, and actionable insights to not only recognize and comprehend dark psychology but to actively counteract and thrive. The journey, while challenging, enlightens and empowers, one revelation at a time.

CHAPTER SIX

Seductive Charms and Invisible Chains: Emotional Manipulation Unveiled

Introduction: The Tug of Heartstrings

Emotions, the profound experiences that give color to our lives, can also become avenues for manipulation. When wielded with ill intent, they can bind stronger than any chain. This chapter delves deep into the intricacies of emotional manipulation, exposing its various facets and exploring methods of protection and recovery.

Emotions: The Dual-Edged Sword

Emotions serve as a compass, guiding us through life. They inform our decisions, shape our relationships, and define our experiences. But this same potency makes them susceptible to exploitation.

Hallmarks of Emotional Manipulation

1. **Gaslighting:** Making someone doubt their reality or memories.
2. **Guilt-tripping:** Making someone feel guilty to control their actions.
3. **Victim Playing:** Manipulators portraying themselves as victims to gain sympathy or concessions.
4. **Love Bombing:** Showering someone with affection and attention only to withdraw it later, creating a cycle of dependency.

In-depth Analysis of Manipulative Techniques

1. Gaslighting: Lighting Illusions

Derived from the play "Gas Light", this technique is a slow eroding of one's confidence in their memory or judgment.

- **Tactics Used:** Denying events, trivializing feelings, or deliberately creating confusion.
- **Impact:** Over time, victims might constantly second-guess themselves, feel anxious, and become increasingly dependent on the manipulator.

2. Guilt-tripping: The Burdened Conscience

Employing guilt as a leash, manipulators ensure compliance or extract favors.

- **Tactics Used:** Bringing up past favors, magnifying one's mistakes, or comparing to others.
- **Impact:** The victim often feels perpetually indebted, anxious about displeasing the manipulator, and trapped in a cycle of repayment.

3. Victim Playing: The Wolf in Sheep's Clothing

By taking on the role of a victim, manipulators disarm and gain undue concessions.

- **Tactics Used:** Exaggerating harm, feigning innocence, or shifting blame.
- **Impact:** Victims often feel defensive, eager to make amends, and constantly walking on eggshells.

4. Love Bombing: The Rollercoaster of Affection

An onslaught of affection creates a powerful bond, which, when withdrawn, leaves the victim craving its return.

- **Tactics Used:** Intense flattery, grand gestures, and creating a "you and me against the world" narrative.
- **Impact:** Victims often feel disoriented during the withdrawal phase, becoming desperate to regain the manipulator's affection, leading to compliance.

Emotional Manipulation in Different Spheres

1. **Personal Relationships:** From friendships to romantic relationships, emotional manipulation can distort the very essence of connection.
2. **Workplace:** From bosses using guilt to extract overtime to colleagues playing victims to evade responsibility.
3. **Societal and Media:** Ad campaigns tapping into fears, peer pressures dictating lifestyles, and media narratives shaping opinions.

The Dance with Dark Triad Traits

- **Narcissists:** Might employ love bombing to get admiration, gaslight to maintain their superior image, and play the victim to avoid accountability.
- **Machiavellians:** Expertly use all forms of emotional manipulation, strategizing for maximum gain.
- **Psychopaths:** While they might not feel emotions deeply, they understand them enough to exploit them in others.

Shields Up: Guarding Against Emotional Manipulation

1. **Awareness:** Recognize the red flags.
2. **Establish Boundaries:** Clearly define what's acceptable and what's not.
3. **Emotional Independence:** Relying on internal validation reduces susceptibility.
4. **Open Communication:** Regularly discussing feelings and concerns with trusted individuals provides clarity.
5. **Professional Help:** Therapists can offer tools and perspectives to heal and safeguard.

Conclusion: Reclaiming Emotional Sovereignty

The journey through the labyrinth of emotional manipulation is challenging but vital. Recognizing the chains, understanding their workings, and learning to break free empowers individuals to reclaim their emotional landscapes.

In subsequent chapters, we will transition from the emotional realm to the physical – exploring how body language, facial expressions, and subtle cues can be avenues of manipulation and control. The quest for understanding and empowerment continues, leading us from darkness to dawn, from vulnerability to resilience.

CHAPTER SEVEN

Silent Echoes: Understanding the Language of Non-Verbal Manipulation

Introduction: Beyond Words

While spoken words play a significant role in our interactions, non-verbal cues often carry more weight than we realize. This silent language of gestures, facial expressions, and body movements can be a treasure trove for manipulators, allowing them to control, deceive, or influence without uttering a single word. This chapter ventures into the intricate maze of non-verbal manipulation, shedding light on its shadows and providing tools to navigate its twists and turns.

The Vocabulary of Silence

Non-verbal communication is diverse, encompassing:

1. **Facial Expressions:** The subtle play of muscles revealing emotions.
2. **Gestures:** The movements of hands, fingers, and arms conveying meanings.
3. **Postures:** The way we sit, stand, or move reflecting our state of mind.
4. **Eye Movements:** From gazes to blinks, the windows to the soul indeed.
5. **Proximity & Touch:** The distance we maintain and the way we touch speaks volumes.
6. **Vocal Tonality & Pitch:** Not what is said, but how it's said.
7. **Dress & Appearance:** Our choices in attire and grooming can be used strategically.

Master Manipulators: Non-Verbal Techniques Employed

1. Mirroring: Imitating another's gestures, postures, or expressions to create rapport.

2. The Power Stance: Dominating physical space to assert authority or control.

3. Prolonged Eye Contact: Maintaining intense eye contact to establish dominance or intimacy.

4. Touch Intrusion: Using touch to establish dominance, intimacy, or instill discomfort.

5. Controlled Facial Expressions: Concealing genuine emotions while displaying fabricated ones.

Breaking Down the Techniques

1. Mirroring:

- **Objective:** Build trust, rapport, or create a sense of similarity.
- **Dark Usage:** Manipulators mirror to make victims lower their guard, making them more susceptible to influence.
- **Countermeasure:** Awareness and subtly altering your body language to see if they adjust accordingly.

2. The Power Stance:

- **Objective:** Display confidence and establish dominance.
- **Dark Usage:** Used to intimidate or overshadow someone's presence.
- **Countermeasure:** Holding one's ground, maintaining eye contact, and not appearing intimidated.

3. Prolonged Eye Contact:

- **Objective:** Connect deeply or establish authority.
- **Dark Usage:** Make someone uncomfortable or force them into submission.
- **Countermeasure:** Breaking the gaze intermittently, or if it becomes too uncomfortable, address it directly.

4. Touch Intrusion:

- **Objective:** Build a connection or assert dominance.
- **Dark Usage:** Unwanted touch can invade personal space, making the victim uncomfortable and submissive.
- **Countermeasure:** Setting clear boundaries and verbalizing discomfort.

5. Controlled Facial Expressions:

- **Objective:** Mask true emotions.
- **Dark Usage:** Hide malicious intent, lie, or mislead.
- **Countermeasure:** Watch for incongruence between words and expressions.

Non-Verbal Cues in Digital Age

In an era of virtual meetings and online interactions, non-verbal cues transition into digital expressions:

- **Profile Choices:** The images, bios, and content chosen can be manipulated to create specific impressions.
- **Emoji & Punctuation Usage:** The digital equivalents of facial expressions and vocal tonality.
- **Video Call Dynamics:** Background choices, camera angles, and lighting can be used to influence perceptions.

Deciphering the Authentic from the Deceptive

- **Baseline Behavior:** Understand an individual's regular non-verbal behavior to spot deviations.
- **Micro-Expressions:** Fleeting facial expressions that reveal genuine emotions.
- **Cluster Analysis:** Look for combinations of non-verbal cues for a clearer picture.

Building a Non-Verbal Defense

1. **Educate Yourself:** Knowledge is the first line of defense.
2. **Practice Observation:** Regularly observe people in various settings.
3. **Trust Your Gut:** Intuition often picks up non-verbal incongruencies.
4. **Establish Boundaries:** Clear boundaries deter most manipulators.

Conclusion: Embracing Empowerment in Silence

Decoding the silent symphony of non-verbal communication not only protects against manipulation but also enriches our interactions. The more attuned we are to this silent language, the more authentic and fulfilling our connections become.

As we journey forward, our exploration deepens, touching upon the societal structures and systems that harbor manipulative mechanisms. The path may be intricate, but with every step, we move closer to clarity, autonomy, and empowerment.

CHAPTER EIGHT

Webs and Echo Chambers: Societal Structures and Manipulative Mechanisms

Introduction: The Subtle Strings of Society

Society, a tapestry woven from collective beliefs, norms, and structures, significantly influences individual behavior and perceptions. However, beneath its visible layers lie intricate webs and echo chambers, often manipulating masses in imperceptible ways. This chapter will pull back the curtains, revealing the manipulative mechanisms embedded within societal structures and offering ways to discern, dissect, and defend against them.

Society's Blueprint: An Overview

Society isn't a monolithic entity but a dynamic structure comprising various components:

1. **Cultural Norms:** Collective beliefs and values that guide behavior.
2. **Media Outlets:** From news agencies to social platforms, they shape perceptions.
3. **Institutional Structures:** Schools, religious bodies, political entities, and more.
4. **Market Forces:** Capitalistic drivers influencing desires and decisions.

The Manipulative Matrix: Where Influence Lies

1. Media Manipulation: How information channels can distort reality.

2. Cultural Conditioning: Unquestioned norms that dictate behavior.

3. Institutional Indoctrination: How institutions can shape mindsets.

4. Consumer Capitalism: The market's invisible hand directing desires.

Diving Deep into the Mechanisms

1. Media Manipulation:

- **Propaganda:** Information, especially of a biased nature, used to promote a political cause or point of view.
- **Selective Reporting:** Choosing to report specific events while ignoring others.
- **Sensationalism:** Using shocking headlines or stories to grab attention.
- **Echo Chambers:** Enclosing oneself in environments where only one's beliefs are echoed back.

2. Cultural Conditioning:

- **Gender Roles:** Prescribed behaviors and expectations based on gender.
- **Status Symbols:** Associating materialistic acquisitions with success.
- **Cultural Taboos:** Unquestioned restrictions rooted in tradition, often controlling behavior through shame.

3. Institutional Indoctrination:

- **Educational Systems:** Curriculum choices shaping worldview.
- **Religious Doctrine:** Dogmatic beliefs discouraging questioning.
- **Political Partisanship:** Fostering blind loyalty to a party, blurring individual reasoning.

4. Consumer Capitalism:

- **Manufactured Needs:** Creating desires for products through advertising.
- **Planned Obsolescence:** Designing products to become obsolete, forcing continued consumption.
- **Celebrity Endorsements:** Using popular figures to influence purchasing decisions.

Societal Influence in the Digital Era

The rise of digital platforms has exponentially magnified societal manipulation:

- **Algorithmic Bubbles:** Online platforms showing content based on user behavior, reinforcing pre-existing beliefs.
- **Misinformation & Fake News:** Unverified information spreading like wildfire.
- **Influencer Culture:** Individuals wielding significant influence, often driven by commercial interests.

Tools for Discernment and Defense

1. **Critical Thinking:** Questioning information rather than accepting it at face value.
2. **Diverse Information Sources:** Avoiding over-reliance on a single media outlet.
3. **Continuous Learning:** Educating oneself about societal structures and their influences.
4. **Mindful Consumption:** Being aware of the forces driving one's purchasing decisions.

Reclaiming Autonomy in a Networked World

While it might seem daunting to navigate a society rife with manipulative mechanisms, awareness and intentionality are powerful allies.

1. **Awareness:** Recognizing manipulation is the first step to counteracting it.
2. **Dialogue:** Engaging in open conversations to understand diverse perspectives.
3. **Self-reflection:** Regular introspection to ensure autonomy in decisions and beliefs.

Conclusion: Navigating the Labyrinth of Society

Society, with its myriad influences, can seem like a complex labyrinth. However, with the right tools and mindset, it's possible to navigate it while retaining one's autonomy. By understanding the manipulative mechanisms at play, individuals can make informed choices, building a society that's more transparent, inclusive, and resilient.

The journey of understanding manipulation now takes a turn inward, exploring the psychological underpinnings that make individuals susceptible to influence and control. As we delve deeper, the quest for empowerment continues, seeking freedom not just externally, but within the recesses of our minds.

CHAPTER NINE

The Mind's Playground: Psychological Vulnerabilities to Manipulation

Introduction: Our Inner Landscape

The human psyche, a realm of emotions, beliefs, and desires, serves as the stage upon which the dance of manipulation is often performed. While external societal structures play a role, understanding the internal vulnerabilities that make us susceptible to manipulation is crucial. This chapter delves deep into the caverns of our minds, shedding light on these vulnerabilities and offering strategies to fortify our mental ramparts.

The Architecture of the Psyche

The human psyche is a complex assembly of:

1. **Emotions:** Our feelings and moods.
2. **Beliefs:** Conceptions we hold about ourselves, others, and the world.
3. **Desires:** Our wants, aspirations, and motivations.
4. **Fears:** What we dread, avoid, or run from.

Unlocking the Doors of Susceptibility

Various aspects of our psyche can be exploited by skilled manipulators:

1. Emotional Dependencies: Reliance on external validation or support.

2. Deep-Seated Fears: Ingrained anxieties or phobias that can be triggered.

3. Unclear Boundaries: Inability to set and maintain personal limits.

4. Cognitive Biases: Mental shortcuts or errors in judgment that can be exploited.

A Deeper Dive into Vulnerabilities

1. Emotional Dependencies:

- **Seeking Validation:** The need for external affirmation can make one malleable to praise or criticism.
- **Fear of Abandonment:** Can make individuals tolerate manipulative relationships.
- **Avoidance of Conflict:** Preferring peace over confrontation, even at personal cost.

2. Deep-Seated Fears:

- **Existential Fears:** Concerns about life's meaning or fear of death can be leveraged by manipulative ideologies or cults.
- **Social Fears:** Fear of exclusion or ostracization can make one conform to manipulative group dynamics.
- **Personal Inadequacies:** Fear of not being 'good enough' can make one susceptible to those who promise improvement or success.

3. Unclear Boundaries:

- **Lack of Self-Worth:** Leads to difficulty in asserting oneself.
- **Past Traumas:** Past experiences can blur one's ability to set healthy boundaries in relationships or situations.

- **Excessive Empathy:** While empathy is valuable, in excess, it can lead to overextending oneself for others, even to one's detriment.

4. Cognitive Biases:

- **Confirmation Bias:** Favoring information that aligns with pre-existing beliefs.
- **Authority Bias:** Over-relying on the opinion of perceived experts or authority figures.
- **Bandwagon Effect:** Conforming to popular opinion or trends without critical examination.

Strengthening the Psyche: Fortification Strategies

1. **Emotional Intelligence:** Recognizing, understanding, and managing our emotions.
2. **Assertiveness Training:** Building the skill to communicate one's needs and rights.
3. **Cognitive Behavioral Therapy (CBT):** Addressing maladaptive patterns of thinking.
4. **Mindfulness & Meditation:** Developing presence and awareness.

Cultivating an Empowered Self-Concept

- **Self-awareness:** Continual reflection to understand one's beliefs, desires, and vulnerabilities.
- **Self-compassion:** Treating oneself with the same kindness and understanding as one would treat a dear friend.
- **Self-efficacy:** Cultivating the belief in one's ability to achieve goals.

Conclusion: Mastering the Inner Realm

Our minds, while being a source of vulnerability, also possess the keys to our empowerment. By understanding our psychological susceptibilities and actively working to address them, we can transform our inner landscape into a sanctuary, impervious to the manipulative tactics of the external world.

As our exploration continues, we will journey into the realm of relationships, dissecting the dynamics of manipulative partnerships and friendships. Equipped with our deepened understanding of the self, we will be better prepared to navigate these interpersonal intricacies and reclaim our agency within them.

CHAPTER TEN

Navigating Treacherous Waters: Dynamics of Manipulative Relationships

Introduction: The Intricacy of Interpersonal Ties

Relationships, the bedrock of human society, form the matrix within which we define our identities, find meaning, and seek fulfillment. However, these connections can sometimes become arenas for manipulation and control, demanding astute awareness and resilience. This chapter charts the multifaceted dimensions of manipulative relationships, offering insights to recognize them and strategies to navigate or even transform such bonds.

The Spectrum of Relationships

Human relationships, diverse in nature, span a range:

1. **Romantic Partnerships:** Bonds of love, commitment, and intimacy.
2. **Familial Ties:** Blood-related or chosen family connections.
3. **Friendships:** Platonic associations based on mutual affection and trust.
4. **Professional Relationships:** Workplace and business-related interactions.

Signposts of Manipulative Dynamics

1. **Unequal Power Dynamics:** One party exerts dominance, controlling the other.

2. **Emotional Blackmail:** Using guilt, anger, or sadness to control behavior.

3. **Gaslighting:** Making someone doubt their perceptions or sanity.

4. **Silent Treatment:** Withholding affection or communication as punishment.

Dissecting the Dynamics

1. Unequal Power Dynamics:

- **Financial Control:** One party controls the monetary resources, undermining the other's independence.
- **Information Withholding:** Keeping vital information hidden to maintain an upper hand.
- **Decision Dominance:** Making major decisions unilaterally, sidelining the other's opinion.

2. Emotional Blackmail:

- **Guilt Tripping:** Making someone feel responsible for the manipulator's unhappiness.
- **Fear Instigation:** Threatening to leave, harm oneself, or retaliate.
- **Obligation Impositions:** Reminding of past favors to extract concessions.

3. Gaslighting:

- **Denying Reality:** Refuting events that have occurred.
- **Trivializing Feelings:** Making the other feel their emotions are overblown or irrational.
- **Shifting Blame:** Turning the tables, making the victim feel they are the problem.

4. Silent Treatment:

- **Emotional Isolation:** Making the person feel alone and undesired.
- **Forced Compliance:** Using silence until the other complies with demands.
- **Creating Dependence:** Making the person crave the manipulator's approval and attention.

Origins of Manipulative Behavior

Understanding the roots of manipulative tendencies can provide clarity:

- **Past Traumas:** Unresolved traumas can drive controlling behaviors.
- **Fear of Abandonment:** Stemming from past betrayals or insecurities.
- **Need for Power:** Possibly arising from feelings of powerlessness in the past.
- **Personality Disorders:** Certain disorders like narcissism can drive manipulative tendencies.

Anchoring Yourself: Strategies to Navigate Manipulative Dynamics

1. **Establish Boundaries:** Clearly define what is acceptable and what isn't.
2. **Seek External Perspectives:** Talk to trusted individuals to gain clarity.
3. **Engage in Self-Care:** Prioritize mental, emotional, and physical well-being.
4. **Consider Professional Help:** Therapy or counseling can offer tools and insights.
5. **Empowerment Through Education:** Understand manipulation techniques to recognize and counteract them.

Reclaiming Relationships: Transformation and Healing

- **Open Communication:** Address concerns and feelings directly.
- **Joint Therapy:** Engaging in couples or family therapy to heal together.
- **Taking Time Apart:** Sometimes, distance can offer clarity and healing.
- **Seeking Community:** Support groups can offer solace and understanding.

Conclusion: Steering the Ship through Stormy Seas

Relationships, while being sources of joy and fulfillment, can also be fraught with challenges. Recognizing and navigating manipulative dynamics ensures that our interpersonal bonds remain rooted in mutual respect, trust, and love. With the tools and understanding we've garnered, we can sail through even the stormiest waters, ensuring our relationships serve as anchors of support, not chains of constraint.

In our next chapter, we will delve into techniques manipulators employ across different contexts, understanding the science behind them, and equipping ourselves to counteract their influence.

CHAPTER ELEVEN

The Machinations of Manipulators: Techniques and Their Underlying Science

Introduction: Unraveling the Craft

Every magician has a set of tricks, and so does every manipulator. The strength of these techniques lies not just in their execution but in the profound understanding of human psychology that underpins them. To truly guard against manipulation, one must not only recognize these techniques but also grasp the science that makes them effective. In this chapter, we dissect the arsenal of manipulators, stripping away the mystique to reveal the machinery at work.

Manipulation: A Fusion of Art and Science

Manipulation, while often viewed with disdain, undeniably marries the creative application of techniques with deep-rooted psychological principles:

1. **Persuasion:** Convincing through argument or appeal.
2. **Deception:** Deliberate presentation of false information.
3. **Influence:** Shaping decisions subtly, often without direct interaction.

Delving into the Toolbox of Manipulation

1. Reciprocity Principle:

- **The Science:** We're wired to repay what's given to us, be it a favor, gift, or gesture.
- **Manipulative Use:** Offering something small (sometimes unsolicited) to create an obligation, expecting a larger return later.
- **Countermeasure:** Recognize the obligation feeling as an innate human response, and evaluate if a reciprocated action is genuinely warranted.

2. Commitment and Consistency:

- **The Science:** We have an inherent desire to remain consistent with our past actions and decisions.
- **Manipulative Use:** Getting a small commitment, which paves the way for larger ones down the line.

- **Countermeasure:** Periodically reassess decisions and commitments, understanding that changing one's mind is a sign of growth, not inconsistency.

3. Social Proof:

- **The Science:** We look to others' behavior to determine our own, especially in uncertain situations.
- **Manipulative Use:** Displaying fake testimonials, endorsements, or staged peer behaviors to sway opinion.
- **Countermeasure:** Seek genuine, independent reviews or feedback, and trust personal experiences and instincts.

4. Liking Principle:

- **The Science:** We're more likely to be persuaded by people we like.
- **Manipulative Use:** Building rapport quickly, mirroring behaviors, or presenting oneself in a relatable manner to exploit this liking.
- **Countermeasure:** Differentiate between liking someone as a person and evaluating their proposal on its merits.

5. Authority Principle:

- **The Science:** We tend to obey authoritative figures or perceived experts even when uncomfortable.
- **Manipulative Use:** Using titles, uniforms, or staged endorsements to give an aura of expertise or authority.

- **Countermeasure:** Question credentials, seek second opinions, and trust your judgment.

6. Scarcity Principle:

- **The Science:** We value things that are scarce more than those in abundance.
- **Manipulative Use:** Creating artificial shortages or time limits to induce urgency.
- **Countermeasure:** Assess if the need is genuine or manufactured. Taking a step back can often offer clarity.

The Neuroscience of Manipulation

Delving deeper, our brain's very wiring makes us susceptible to these tactics:

- **Amygdala:** Processes emotions like fear, which can be triggered by tactics like scarcity.
- **Pre-frontal Cortex:** Responsible for reasoning, it can be bypassed by manipulative emotional appeals.
- **Mirror Neurons:** They make us empathize and mirror others, a fact exploited by the liking principle.

Crafting a Shield: Building Resistance

1. **Education:** A fundamental understanding of manipulation techniques is the first step.
2. **Critical Thinking:** Evaluate information for its source, context, and logic.
3. **Emotional Awareness:** Recognize and regulate emotional responses to ensure they don't cloud judgment.

4. **Seeking Feedback:** Sharing decisions with trusted confidants can provide alternative viewpoints.

Conclusion: Mastery over Mystery

Manipulation, while formidable, loses much of its power when we demystify its techniques and the science behind them. Armed with knowledge, self-awareness, and a network of trusted allies, we can navigate the world with a renewed sense of agency and confidence.

As we venture forward, our exploration will shift from defense to offense. Chapter 12 will introduce us to positive persuasion, where we learn to ethically influence and inspire others, harnessing the very principles that manipulators misuse, but for benevolent ends.

CHAPTER TWELVE

Ethical Elevation: The Art of Positive Persuasion

Introduction: Harnessing Power for the Greater Good

Manipulation's shadow need not dim the light of positive persuasion. Where manipulation seeks control, persuasion seeks understanding. Where manipulation imposes, persuasion proposes. This chapter delves deep into the realm of ethical influence, illustrating how the tools often used for deceit can be refashioned into instruments of inspiration, collaboration, and positive change.

The Ethical Imperative: Drawing the Line

Before diving into the techniques, it's crucial to differentiate manipulation from ethical persuasion:

1. **Intent:** Positive persuasion is driven by a genuine belief in mutual benefit.
2. **Transparency:** The process and purpose are clear and open to scrutiny.
3. **Respect for Autonomy:** Persuasion offers information and choice, rather than removing agency.

The Principles of Positive Persuasion

1. Genuine Reciprocity:

- **The Ethical Approach:** Offer genuine value without expecting anything in return.
- **Impact:** Builds trust and goodwill, forming the basis for long-term relationships.
- **Real-world Application:** Businesses offering valuable content or services for free to genuinely help potential customers.

2. Authentic Commitment:

- **The Ethical Approach:** Encourage commitments that align with personal values and beliefs.
- **Impact:** Fosters intrinsic motivation and lasting behavioral change.
- **Real-world Application:** Social campaigns that invite people to pledge for causes they genuinely care about.

3. True Social Proof:

- **The Ethical Approach:** Showcase genuine endorsements, testimonials, and peer behaviors.
- **Impact:** Creates a legitimate community feel, promoting genuine products or ideals.
- **Real-world Application:** Crowdfunding platforms where the community genuinely backs a product or cause.

4. Building Real Rapport:

- **The Ethical Approach:** Foster connections based on genuine interest and mutual respect.
- **Impact:** Lays the foundation for collaborative partnerships.
- **Real-world Application:** Effective networking where connections are nurtured over time, not just transactionally.

5. Ethical Authority:

- **The Ethical Approach:** Earn authority through expertise, integrity, and consistent action.
- **Impact:** Guides and inspires others based on genuine credibility.
- **Real-world Application:** Thought leaders who have earned their position through consistent value addition and expertise.

6. Honest Scarcity:

- **The Ethical Approach:** Be transparent about genuine limitations without creating artificial urgency.
- **Impact:** Fosters trust and encourages action based on real constraints.
- **Real-world Application:** Limited-time offers based on actual stock or capacity limitations.

Psychological Mechanisms at Play

Understanding the mind's workings can enhance the efficacy of ethical persuasion:

- **Cognitive Dissonance:** People prefer their beliefs and actions to align. Ethical persuasion ensures this alignment is positive.
- **Confirmation Bias:** We favor information that confirms our beliefs. Positive persuasion presents data that supports beneficial beliefs.
- **The Halo Effect:** Our overall impression of someone influences our feelings about their attributes. Genuine, positive actions create a favorable halo.

Crafting a Message: The Pillars of Ethical Influence

1. **Clarity:** Be straightforward. Avoid jargon or overly complex explanations.
2. **Authenticity:** Be genuine in intent and delivery.
3. **Emotional Resonance:** Connect with the audience's feelings and values.
4. **Actionability:** Make it easy for the audience to act on the persuasion.

Conclusion: The Legacy of Positive Persuasion

As we've journeyed through the landscape of influence, we've seen its dual faces: the shadowy recesses of manipulation and the sunlit peaks of positive persuasion. By choosing the ethical path, we not only uplift ourselves but also those we interact with, leaving a legacy of trust, collaboration, and positive change.

In Chapter 13, we will journey further into the realm of building trust, an essential cornerstone for any meaningful interaction or transaction, ensuring our endeavors are not only successful but also deeply fulfilling.

CHAPTER THIRTEEN

Foundations of Faith: Building and Nurturing Trust in a Skeptical World

Introduction: The Pillar of All Relations

In the intricate dance of human interactions, if there's one element that stands as the bedrock, it's trust. Whether personal or professional, no meaningful relationship can thrive without this fundamental element. Yet, as indispensable as trust is, it remains a delicate entity, easy to break and arduous to build. In this pivotal chapter, we delve into the profound importance of trust, the science behind it, and the path to fostering it in an increasingly distrustful world.

The Value of Trust: Beyond the Intangible

Trust isn't merely a feel-good factor; its value has tangible implications:

1. **Efficiency:** Trust eliminates the need for constant monitoring and verification, streamlining interactions.
2. **Collaboration:** High trust levels enable open sharing of information, fostering collaboration and innovation.
3. **Resilience:** Trustworthy relationships can weather storms and recover from setbacks more effectively.

The Neurology of Trust

Trust isn't just a philosophical concept; it has roots in our very biology:

- **Oxytocin:** Often dubbed the "trust hormone," increased oxytocin levels have been linked to more trusting behaviors.
- **Amygdala:** This part of our brain assesses threats and plays a role in deciding whether someone is trustworthy.
- **Anterior Cingulate Cortex:** Involved in error detection, it helps us recognize when our trust is misplaced.

The Trust Equation: Components of Trustworthiness

Drawing from the domain of organizational psychology, trust can be distilled into four key components:

1. **Credibility:** Does the person have the knowledge and skills they claim to have?
2. **Reliability:** Can we count on this person to do what they say they will?
3. **Intimacy:** Do we feel safe sharing personal information or concerns with this person?
4. **Self-Orientation:** Is this person's primary concern their own interests or those of others?

Trustworthiness = (Credibility + Reliability + Intimacy) / Self-Orientation

The Stages of Trust Building

1. Establishment:

- The starting phase where first impressions play a crucial role.
- Key actions: Displaying competence, being punctual, offering genuine assistance.

2. Verification:

- Observing actions over time to validate initial assessments.
- Key actions: Consistency in behavior, fulfilling promises, transparent communication.

3. Deepening:

- Moving beyond surface interactions to develop a deeper connection.
- Key actions: Sharing vulnerabilities, active listening, displaying empathy.

4. Sustenance:

- Maintaining trust over extended periods.
- Key actions: Continual open communication, acknowledging errors, making amends when necessary.

Restoring Broken Trust

1. **Acknowledgment:** Accept and admit the breach without deflecting.
2. **Understanding:** Dive deep to understand the implications of the breach.
3. **Apology:** Genuine remorse, devoid of excuses.
4. **Amends:** Concrete actions to rectify the situation.
5. **Consistency:** Repeated trustworthy behavior over time to rebuild faith.

Practical Steps for Trust Building in the Digital Age

- **Digital Footprint:** Ensure consistency between online persona and real-life behavior.
- **Transparency:** Clearly state intentions, especially in transactions or data collection.
- **Engagement:** Regularly interact with peers, customers, or followers, showcasing authenticity.

Conclusion: The Enduring Elixir of Trust

In an era where skepticism often reigns supreme, the currency of trust has never been more valuable. By understanding its intricate nuances and actively working towards fostering it, we not only enrich our personal and professional relationships but also create ripples of positivity in the wider world.

As we transition to Chapter 14, we'll explore how to harness trust in leadership, ensuring not just compliance but genuine allegiance and dedication, elevating our collective endeavors to unprecedented heights.

CHAPTER FOURTEEN

Leading with Trust: The Heartbeat of Authentic Leadership

Introduction: The Imperative of Trust-Centered Leadership

At the confluence of power, responsibility, and influence lies leadership. Yet, true leadership transcends titles or designations; it's rooted in the intangible bond of trust. As we sail into the turbulent waters of the 21st century, characterized by rapid technological advancements and ever-shifting socio-political landscapes, trust-centered leadership emerges not just as a preference, but as a vital necessity.

The Historical Context: Leadership and Trust Through the Ages

To understand the profound bond between leadership and trust, we must journey back in time:

- **Ancient Tribes:** Leaders were often chosen based on their ability to protect the tribe and make decisions in its best interest.
- **Medieval Monarchies:** Loyalty was ensured through fear and might, but the most enduring monarchies were those where the populace genuinely trusted their ruler's judgment.
- **Modern Democracies:** Elected representatives are entrusted with the power to lead based on promises and past records, making trust a pivotal cornerstone.

The Trust Deficit: Modern Leadership Challenges

In our current era, several factors challenge the traditional paradigms of leadership:

1. **Information Overload:** The digital age brings a deluge of information, leading to skepticism and mistrust.
2. **Past Betrayals:** Historical instances of leaders abusing power have left scars.
3. **Impersonal Interactions:** Digital interactions often lack the personal touch, making trust-building more challenging.

The Four Pillars of Trust-Centered Leadership

1. Authenticity: Being Real in a World of Facades

- **Vulnerability:** Authentic leaders aren't afraid to showcase their humanity, admitting mistakes and sharing personal anecdotes.
- **Consistency:** Aligning words with actions, ensuring there's no disconnect between public and private personas.

2. Transparency: Letting Light Into the Shadows

- **Open Communication:** Encouraging an open-door policy, where concerns and suggestions are welcomed.
- **Clear Intentions:** Declaring objectives openly, eliminating any room for doubt or speculation.

3. Empathy: Walking in Others' Shoes

- **Active Listening:** Giving undivided attention, not just to words, but to emotions and underlying concerns.
- **Genuine Care:** Beyond professional responsibilities, showing interest in the personal well-being of team members or followers.

4. Reliability: Becoming the Anchor in Stormy Seas

- **Follow-Through:** Ensuring that promises are not empty words but are followed by actions.
- **Steadfastness:** Displaying calm and consistency, especially in challenging situations.

Practical Tools for Trust Building in Leadership

- **Feedback Mechanisms:** Regularly collecting and addressing feedback, showcasing a commitment to improvement.
- **Collaborative Decision Making:** Involving team members or stakeholders in major decisions, validating their expertise and perspective.
- **Education and Training:** Investing in continuous learning, displaying commitment to growth and adaptability.

Leading by Example: Trust-Centered Leadership in Action

Highlighting real-world examples, from corporate magnates who've prioritized employee well-being, to political leaders whose authenticity won hearts, showcasing that trust-centered leadership isn't just a theory but a tangible, practical approach with proven results.

Conclusion: The Ripple Effect of Trust-Centered Leadership

Trust, while intangible, has palpable effects. When leaders prioritize trust, they not only elevate their immediate teams or organizations but set in motion a ripple effect, shaping industries, societies, and, eventually, the very fabric of human interactions. Such leaders don't just lead; they inspire, transforming the very essence of what leadership stands for.

As we journey to Chapter 15, we'll explore how trust plays a pivotal role in team dynamics, ensuring that groups don't just function, but thrive, fostering creativity, innovation, and unparalleled synergy.

CHAPTER FIFTEEN

Trust in Teams: The Crucible of Collective Triumph

Introduction: The Symphony of Synergy

Picture a symphony orchestra. Every instrument, from the imposing double bass to the delicate piccolo, contributes to the musical tapestry. Yet, it's the invisible bond of trust between the musicians that transforms individual notes into an enthralling melody. Similarly, in the realm of human collaboration, teams are the orchestras, and trust is the invisible maestro, guiding them towards unparalleled harmony and success.

The Evolutionary Perspective: Trust as a Survival Mechanism

Before delving into the complexities of modern teams, let's embark on a journey to the primordial savannas where our ancestors roamed:

- **Hunting in Packs:** The early human's ability to trust and collaborate was key to hunting large prey, ensuring shared nourishment and survival.
- **Division of Labor:** As tribes evolved, roles diversified. The hunter trusted the gatherer, and the artisan trusted the warrior, creating a web of interdependence.
- **Shared Narratives:** Campfire stories and cave paintings were early testimonials of shared experiences and mutual trust.

Modern Team Dynamics: Beyond Group Work

In today's fast-paced, globalized world, the essence of teams has undergone a seismic shift:

1. **Diversity of Skills:** Teams now comprise members with specialized skills, mirroring the division of labor in ancient tribes but on a more intricate scale.
2. **Virtual Teams:** Geographic boundaries have dissolved, making trust even more crucial in the age of digital collaboration.
3. **Interdisciplinary Collaboration:** Different sectors and industries often merge their expertise, weaving a tapestry of shared goals and mutual trust.

Five Layers of Trust in Team Dynamics

1. Individual Trustworthiness:

- Every team member's reliability, transparency, and authenticity.
- Building personal rapport, showcasing commitment through actions.

2. Interpersonal Trust:

- The trust between two team members.
- Fostered through open communication, understanding, and mutual respect.

3. Team-wide Trust:

- A collective sense of reliability and cohesion.
- Built via team-building exercises, shared successes, and navigating challenges together.

4. Trust in Leadership:

- Team members' faith in their leaders or managers.
- Leaders play a crucial role by being approachable, transparent, and leading by example.

5. External Trust:

- The trust between the team and external stakeholders or clients.
- Ensured through consistent deliverables, open communication, and meeting, if not exceeding, expectations.

Tools and Techniques to Foster Trust in Teams

- **Regular Check-ins:** Frequent touchpoints to discuss not just tasks but feelings, concerns, and aspirations.
- **Conflict Resolution Protocols:** Clear mechanisms to address and resolve conflicts, emphasizing understanding and growth.
- **Collaborative Platforms:** Using technology to bridge gaps, ensuring transparent task management and open channels of communication.

Trust Busters: Pitfalls to Avoid

1. **Ambiguity:** Lack of clarity in roles, objectives, or feedback.
2. **Micromanagement:** Overbearing oversight stifles autonomy and displays a lack of trust.
3. **Inequity:** Perceived or real favoritism or discrimination erodes the trust foundation.

Trust Multipliers: Catalysts for Enhanced Team Trust

1. **Celebrating Small Wins:** Regularly acknowledging and celebrating achievements, fostering a sense of shared success.
2. **Transparency in Failures:** Instead of finger-pointing, collaboratively learning from mistakes.
3. **Personal Growth Opportunities:** Investing in team members' growth, showcasing long-term commitment and care.

Case Studies: Trust-Driven Team Triumphs

Highlighting real-world instances from diverse sectors—from a tech startup's journey from a garage to Silicon Valley, guided by mutual trust, to a humanitarian group's endeavors in crisis zones, powered by undying faith in each other.

Conclusion: The Timeless Tapestry of Trust

In a world where the only constant is change, the trust-based teams stand as timeless testimonies to human potential. Their triumphs aren't just achievements but landmarks in the unending journey of human collaboration and evolution.

CONCLUSION

As we draw the curtains on this illuminating journey through the labyrinth of dark psychology, manipulation, and the redemptive power of trust, it becomes evident that human psyche, with its intricacies and contradictions, is akin to a vast ocean, both serene and stormy. This expedition was not merely academic; it was an exploration of the very core of what makes us human, delving deep into the shadows of manipulation, only to emerge into the radiant realm of trust and authenticity.

The Duality of Our Nature

At the heart of this narrative lies an understanding of our dual nature. We possess the capacity for manipulation and deceit, but we also have an innate propensity for trust, cooperation, and altruism. Our journey through the chapters showcased that while dark psychology provides insights into manipulation tactics and their profound impacts, it also underscores the significance of genuine human connections, anchored in trust.

Knowledge as Empowerment

Understanding dark psychology is not about endorsing manipulation, but about empowerment. When armed with knowledge, individuals are better equipped to recognize manipulation, guard against its influences, and make informed decisions. As the old adage goes, "forewarned is forearmed."

Trust as the Beacon

In the vast sea of human interactions, trust stands as the beacon that guides ships safely to the shore. As elucidated in the latter chapters, trust is not just a feel-good factor but the very foundation of successful relationships, teams, and societies. Whether in the personal realm or the vast expanse of leadership and organizations, trust emerges as the crucible of collective success and well-being.

The Way Forward

Awareness of dark psychology coupled with an understanding of trust provides a balanced toolkit for the modern individual. It's like having a compass that warns of treacherous terrains while also pointing towards safer paths. But knowledge alone is passive; its true power is unlocked when coupled with action:

1. **Continual Learning:** The realms of psychology, human behavior, and interpersonal dynamics are continually evolving. Staying updated ensures proactive preparedness.
2. **Open Conversations:** Talking about dark psychology and manipulation, raising awareness, and sharing experiences can demystify and diminish their negative impacts.
3. **Building Trust-Centered Communities:** Encouraging environments where trust is valued, nurtured, and celebrated can serve as bulwarks against the shadows of manipulation.

Parting Thoughts

As we close this book, let it not be the end but the beginning —of awareness, of conversations, of personal and collective journeys towards a world where understanding reigns supreme, where the shadows of manipulation are dispelled by the radiant glow of trust.

In this complex dance of life, may we always remember that while we might occasionally stumble upon the dark, it's the light that defines our path, our purpose, and our true essence. Let's cherish this light, protect it, and pass it on, ensuring that the legacy we leave is one of enlightenment, empowerment, and enduring trust.